Sweet Twist

The Churros Candy Bars Cookbook

SWEET TWIST

First edition. March 15, 2024.

Copyright © 2024 Jose Maria.

ISBN: 979-8224129607

Written by Jose Maria.

Table of Contents

Jose Maria

❖ Introduction

A. Welcome to the World of Churros Candy Bars

Welcome, fellow dessert enthusiasts, to the delightful fusion of two beloved treats: churros and candy bars. In this culinary adventure, we'll explore the tantalizing world where crispy, cinnamon-sugar coated churros meet the sweet indulgence of candy bars. Get ready to embark on a journey filled with mouthwatering flavors, innovative creations, and irresistible treats that will satisfy your sweet tooth like never before.

B. History and Origins of Churros and Candy Bars

To truly appreciate the magic of churros candy bars, it's essential to understand the rich history and origins of these iconic desserts. Churros, believed to have originated in Spain centuries ago, were traditionally enjoyed as a breakfast pastry or a snack paired with chocolate sauce. Over time, they have become a beloved treat worldwide, with each culture adding its own unique twist.

On the other hand, candy bars have a more recent history, with their origins dating back to the late 19th century. These convenient confections quickly gained popularity, offering a convenient way to satisfy cravings for something sweet on the go.

Now, imagine combining the crispy, doughy goodness of churros with the irresistible allure of candy bars – it's a match made in dessert heaven!

C. Ingredients Overview and Essential Tools

Before diving into the recipes, let's familiarize ourselves with the essential ingredients and tools needed to create these delectable churros candy bars.

Ingredients:

1. Flour: All-purpose flour is typically used as the base for churros dough.
2. Sugar: Both granulated sugar and powdered sugar are used for coating and sweetening.
3. Butter: Adds richness and flavor to the churros dough.
4. Eggs: Provide structure and moisture to the dough.
5. Spices: Cinnamon and other spices add warmth and depth of flavor.
6. Chocolate: For dipping, drizzling, or filling, depending on the recipe.
7. Caramel: Adds a decadent, gooey texture to certain variations.
8. Peanut Butter, Jam, or other fillings: Enhance the flavor and texture of stuffed churros.
9. Matcha, Raspberry, Dulce de Leche, or other flavorings: Used to infuse unique flavors into churros.

Essential Tools:

- Heavy-bottomed saucepan or deep fryer: For frying the churros.
- Piping bag fitted with a star tip: To pipe the churros dough into the desired shapes.
- Slotted spoon or spider strainer: For removing the fried churros from the oil.
- Baking sheets lined with parchment paper: To cool and drain the churros.
- Mixing bowls, whisk, and spatula: For preparing the churros

dough and coatings.

- Now that we have our ingredients and tools ready, it's time to unleash our creativity and indulge in the sweet magic of churros candy bars!

D. Tips for Perfecting Churros Candy Bars

Creating the perfect churros candy bars requires attention to detail and a few expert tips to ensure success every time:

1. Maintain the right dough consistency: The churros dough should be smooth and pipeable but not too runny or stiff. Adjust the flour and liquid ratio as needed to achieve the perfect consistency.

2. Preheat the oil to the correct temperature: For crispy churros with a golden exterior, preheat the oil to around 350°F (175°C). Use a candy thermometer to monitor the temperature and adjust the heat accordingly.

3. Pipe uniform shapes: Consistency is key when piping the churros dough onto the baking sheet. Keep the pressure steady to ensure uniform shapes and sizes, which will result in even frying.

4. Don't overcrowd the frying pan: Fry the churros in batches to prevent overcrowding, which can lower the oil temperature and result in soggy churros.

5. Coat while warm: Roll the freshly fried churros in cinnamon sugar or other coatings while they are still warm to ensure that the coating adheres properly and adds maximum flavor.

6. Experiment with fillings and toppings: Get creative with your churros candy bars by experimenting with different fillings, toppings, and dipping sauces. From chocolate and caramel to fruit jams and nut butters, the possibilities are endless!

With these tips in mind, you're well-equipped to embark on your churros candy bar adventure. Get ready to impress friends and family with your delicious creations!

Chapter (1) Classic Churros Candy Bars

A. Traditional Churros with Chocolate Drizzle
   Ingredients:

- 1 cup water
- 2 tablespoons white sugar
- 1/2 teaspoon salt
- 2 tablespoons vegetable oil
- 1 cup all-purpose flour
- Vegetable oil, for frying
- 1/4 cup granulated sugar
- 1 teaspoon ground cinnamon
- 1/2 cup semi-sweet chocolate chips
- 2 tablespoons heavy cream

Instructions:

1. In a saucepan over medium heat, combine water, sugar, salt, and vegetable oil. Bring the mixture to a boil.
2. Remove the saucepan from the heat and stir in the flour until the mixture forms a dough.
3. Heat vegetable oil in a deep skillet or pot over medium-high heat until it reaches 350°F (175°C).
4. Transfer the dough to a piping bag fitted with a star tip.
5. Carefully pipe 4-6 inch strips of dough directly into the hot oil, using scissors to cut the dough.
6. Fry the churros until they are golden brown and crispy, about 2-3 minutes per side. Use a slotted spoon to transfer them to a paper towel-lined plate to drain excess oil.
7. In a shallow dish, combine granulated sugar and ground cinnamon. Roll the warm churros in the cinnamon sugar

mixture until evenly coated.

8. In a microwave-safe bowl, combine chocolate chips and heavy cream. Microwave in 30-second intervals, stirring each time, until the chocolate is melted and smooth.
9. Drizzle the melted chocolate over the cinnamon sugar-coated churros.
10. Serve the traditional churros with chocolate drizzle immediately and enjoy!

B. Cinnamon Sugar-Coated Churros with Caramel Sauce
Ingredients:

- Prepared churros from the previous recipe
- 1/2 cup granulated sugar
- 1 teaspoon ground cinnamon
- 1/2 cup caramel sauce (store-bought or homemade)

Instructions:

1. Follow steps 7-8 from the previous recipe to prepare the cinnamon sugar-coated churros.
2. Warm the caramel sauce in a saucepan over low heat or in the microwave until it's pourable.
3. Drizzle the warm caramel sauce over the cinnamon sugar-coated churros.
4. Serve immediately, and enjoy the irresistible combination of crispy churros and gooey caramel!

C. Classic Churros Stuffed with Creamy Peanut Butter
Ingredients:

- Prepared churros dough from the previous recipe
- Creamy peanut butter

Instructions:

1. Prepare the churros dough and pipe them into 4-6 inch strips as described in the previous recipe.
2. Transfer the peanut butter to a piping bag fitted with a small round tip.
3. Carefully insert the piping tip into the center of each churro and pipe a generous amount of peanut butter into the center.
4. Fry the stuffed churros until golden brown and crispy, following the frying instructions from the previous recipe.
5. Drain excess oil from the churros on a paper towel-lined plate.
6. Serve the stuffed churros warm and enjoy the delightful combination of crispy dough and creamy peanut butter filling!

These classic churros candy bars are sure to delight your taste buds with their irresistible flavors and textures. Enjoy them as a special treat any time of the day!

Chapter (2) Creative Variations

A. Matcha Infused Churros with White Chocolate Ganache

Ingredients:

- 1 cup water
- 2 tablespoons white sugar
- 1/2 teaspoon salt
- 2 tablespoons vegetable oil
- 1 tablespoon matcha powder
- 1 cup all-purpose flour
- Vegetable oil, for frying
- 1/4 cup granulated sugar
- 1 teaspoon matcha powder (for dusting)
- 1/2 cup white chocolate chips
- 1/4 cup heavy cream

Instructions:

1. In a saucepan over medium heat, combine water, sugar, salt, vegetable oil, and 1 tablespoon of matcha powder. Bring the mixture to a boil.
2. Remove the saucepan from the heat and stir in the flour until the mixture forms a smooth dough.
3. Transfer the dough to a piping bag fitted with a star tip.
4. Heat vegetable oil in a deep skillet or pot over medium-high heat until it reaches 350°F (175°C).
5. Carefully pipe 4-6 inch strips of dough directly into the hot oil, using scissors to cut the dough.
6. Fry the churros until they are golden brown and crispy, about 2-3 minutes per side. Use a slotted spoon to transfer them to a paper towel-lined plate to drain excess oil.

7. In a shallow dish, combine granulated sugar and 1 teaspoon of matcha powder. Roll the warm churros in the matcha sugar mixture until evenly coated.

8. In a microwave-safe bowl, combine white chocolate chips and heavy cream. Microwave in 30-second intervals, stirring each time, until the chocolate is melted and smooth.

9. Serve the matcha-infused churros with white chocolate ganache for dipping. Enjoy the delightful combination of earthy matcha and creamy white chocolate!

B. Raspberry Jam-Filled Churros with Dark Chocolate Dipping Sauce

Ingredients:

- Prepared churros dough from the previous recipe
- Raspberry jam
- Vegetable oil, for frying
- 1/2 cup dark chocolate chips
- 1/4 cup heavy cream

Instructions:

1. Prepare the churros dough and pipe them into 4-6 inch strips as described in the previous recipe.

2. Transfer the raspberry jam to a piping bag fitted with a small round tip.

3. Carefully insert the piping tip into the center of each churro and pipe a generous amount of raspberry jam into the center.

4. Fry the filled churros until golden brown and crispy, following the frying instructions from the previous recipe.

5. Drain excess oil from the churros on a paper towel-lined plate.

6. In a microwave-safe bowl, combine dark chocolate chips and heavy cream. Microwave in 30-second intervals, stirring each

time, until the chocolate is melted and smooth.

7. Serve the raspberry jam-filled churros with dark chocolate dipping sauce. Enjoy the burst of fruity flavor paired with rich dark chocolate!

C. Spiced Churros with Dulce de Leche Swirl

Ingredients:

- 1 cup water
- 2 tablespoons white sugar
- 1/2 teaspoon salt
- 2 tablespoons vegetable oil
- 1 teaspoon ground cinnamon
- 1/4 teaspoon ground nutmeg
- 1/4 teaspoon ground cloves
- 1 cup all-purpose flour
- Vegetable oil, for frying
- 1/4 cup granulated sugar
- 1/2 cup dulce de leche

Instructions:

1. In a saucepan over medium heat, combine water, sugar, salt, vegetable oil, and spices (cinnamon, nutmeg, and cloves). Bring the mixture to a boil.
2. Remove the saucepan from the heat and stir in the flour until the mixture forms a smooth dough.
3. Transfer the dough to a piping bag fitted with a star tip.
4. Heat vegetable oil in a deep skillet or pot over medium-high heat until it reaches 350°F (175°C).
5. Carefully pipe 4-6 inch strips of dough directly into the hot oil, using scissors to cut the dough.
6. Fry the churros until they are golden brown and crispy, about

2-3 minutes per side. Use a slotted spoon to transfer them to a paper towel-lined plate to drain excess oil.

7. In a shallow dish, combine granulated sugar and a pinch of ground cinnamon. Roll the warm churros in the spiced sugar mixture until evenly coated.

8. Transfer dulce de leche to a piping bag fitted with a small round tip.

9. Drizzle the dulce de leche over the spiced churros in a swirling pattern.

10. Serve the spiced churros with dulce de leche swirl immediately and savor the warm, comforting flavors of cinnamon, nutmeg, cloves, and caramel!

Chapter (3) Churros Candy Bar Mashups

A. Churros S'mores Bars

Ingredients:

- Prepared churros dough from the previous recipe
- 1 cup mini marshmallows
- 1/2 cup chocolate chips
- 1/2 cup crushed graham crackers

Instructions:

1. Prepare the churros dough and pipe them into a square baking dish, forming a single layer.
2. Bake the churros according to the recipe instructions until golden brown and crispy.
3. Sprinkle mini marshmallows, chocolate chips, and crushed graham crackers evenly over the baked churros.
4. Return the baking dish to the oven and bake for an additional 5-7 minutes, or until the marshmallows are golden and gooey.
5. Remove from the oven and let cool slightly before slicing into bars.
6. Serve the churros s'mores bars warm and enjoy the delicious combination of crispy churros, melted chocolate, and gooey marshmallows!

B. Churros Cheesecake Bars with Salted Caramel Drizzle
Ingredients:

- Prepared churros dough from the previous recipe
- 8 oz cream cheese, softened
- 1/4 cup granulated sugar
- 1 egg
- 1 teaspoon vanilla extract
- 1/2 cup salted caramel sauce (store-bought or homemade)

Instructions:

1. Prepare the churros dough and press it into the bottom of a greased square baking dish, forming a single layer.
2. In a mixing bowl, beat together the softened cream cheese, granulated sugar, egg, and vanilla extract until smooth and creamy.
3. Spread the cream cheese mixture evenly over the churros dough in the baking dish.
4. Bake in a preheated oven at 350°F (175°C) for 25-30 minutes, or until the cheesecake layer is set and the edges are golden brown.
5. Let the cheesecake bars cool completely, then drizzle with salted caramel sauce.
6. Slice into bars and serve chilled or at room temperature. Enjoy the indulgent combination of creamy cheesecake, crispy churros, and rich salted caramel!

C. Churros Brownie Bites with Fudge Frosting

Ingredients:

- Prepared churros dough from the previous recipe
- Prepared brownie batter (store-bought or homemade)
- 1/2 cup chocolate chips
- 1/4 cup heavy cream

Instructions:

1. Prepare the churros dough and pipe them into mini muffin cups, filling each cup halfway.
2. Spoon brownie batter on top of the churros dough in each muffin cup, filling them almost to the top.
3. Bake in a preheated oven according to the brownie recipe instructions until the brownies are cooked through.
4. While the brownie bites are baking, prepare the fudge frosting by combining chocolate chips and heavy cream in a microwave-safe bowl. Microwave in 30-second intervals, stirring each time, until the chocolate is melted and smooth.
5. Once the brownie bites are done baking, let them cool slightly before drizzling with the fudge frosting.
6. Serve the churros brownie bites with fudge frosting and enjoy the heavenly combination of rich chocolate brownies and crispy churros!

Chapter (4) Vegan and Gluten-Free Options

A. Vegan Churros with Dairy-Free Chocolate Sauce
Ingredients for Vegan Churros:

- 1 cup water
- 2 tablespoons vegetable oil
- 2 tablespoons white sugar
- 1/2 teaspoon salt
- 1 cup all-purpose flour
- Vegetable oil, for frying

Ingredients for Dairy-Free Chocolate Sauce:

- 1/2 cup dairy-free chocolate chips
- 1/4 cup coconut cream (the solid part from a can of full-fat coconut milk)
- 1 tablespoon maple syrup (optional, for sweetness)

Instructions for Vegan Churros:

1. In a saucepan, combine water, vegetable oil, sugar, and salt. Bring to a boil over medium heat.
2. Remove from heat and stir in the flour until the mixture forms a smooth dough.
3. Transfer the dough to a piping bag fitted with a star tip.
4. Heat vegetable oil in a deep skillet or pot over medium-high heat until it reaches 350°F (175°C).
5. Carefully pipe 4-6 inch strips of dough directly into the hot oil, using scissors to cut the dough.
6. Fry the churros until they are golden brown and crispy, about 2-3 minutes per side. Use a slotted spoon to transfer them to a

paper towel-lined plate to drain excess oil.

Instructions for Dairy-Free Chocolate Sauce:

1. In a microwave-safe bowl, combine dairy-free chocolate chips and coconut cream.
2. Microwave in 30-second intervals, stirring each time, until the chocolate is melted and smooth.
3. Stir in maple syrup if desired for sweetness.
4. Serve the vegan churros with dairy-free chocolate sauce for dipping. Enjoy the delicious combination guilt-free!

B. Gluten-Free Churros Cookie Bars
Ingredients:

- 1 cup gluten-free all-purpose flour
- 1 cup water
- 2 tablespoons vegetable oil
- 2 tablespoons white sugar
- 1/2 teaspoon salt
- 1/2 teaspoon ground cinnamon
- 1/2 cup granulated sugar (for coating)
- 1 teaspoon ground cinnamon (for coating)

Instructions:

1. Preheat your oven to 350°F (175°C) and grease a square baking dish.
2. In a saucepan, combine water, vegetable oil, sugar, salt, and cinnamon. Bring to a boil over medium heat.
3. Remove from heat and stir in the gluten-free flour until the mixture forms a smooth dough.
4. Press the dough evenly into the prepared baking dish.
5. Bake in the preheated oven for 25-30 minutes, or until the edges

are golden brown and the center is set.

6. In a shallow dish, combine granulated sugar and ground cinnamon for coating.

7. While still warm, cut the baked churros cookie bars into squares and roll them in the cinnamon sugar mixture until coated.

8. Serve the gluten-free churros cookie bars warm or at room temperature and savor the cinnamon-spiced goodness!

C. Coconut Milk Caramel Vegan Churros
Ingredients for Vegan Churros:

- 1 cup water
- 2 tablespoons vegetable oil
- 2 tablespoons white sugar
- 1/2 teaspoon salt
- 1 cup all-purpose flour
- Vegetable oil, for frying

Ingredients for Coconut Milk Caramel Sauce:

- 1 can (13.5 oz) full-fat coconut milk
- 1 cup brown sugar
- 1/2 teaspoon vanilla extract
- Pinch of salt

Instructions for Vegan Churros:

- Follow the instructions for vegan churros provided in the previous recipe.

Instructions for Coconut Milk Caramel Sauce:

1. In a saucepan, combine coconut milk and brown sugar over medium heat.

2. Bring the mixture to a simmer, stirring frequently.
3. Cook for about 10-15 minutes, or until the sauce thickens and turns a deep caramel color.
4. Remove from heat and stir in vanilla extract and a pinch of salt.
5. Let the caramel sauce cool slightly before serving with the vegan churros.
6. Serve the vegan churros with coconut milk caramel sauce for dipping. Enjoy the luscious caramel flavor with a hint of coconut goodness!

Chapter (5) Churros Candy Bar Dessert Hacks

A. Churros Ice Cream Sandwiches
Ingredients:

- Prepared churros from the previous recipe
- Vanilla ice cream

Instructions:

1. Allow the prepared churros to cool slightly but still remain warm.
2. Slice the churros in half horizontally to create top and bottom pieces for the sandwich.
3. Place a scoop of vanilla ice cream onto the bottom half of each churro.
4. Gently press the top half of the churro onto the ice cream to form a sandwich.
5. Serve immediately or wrap each sandwich in parchment paper and freeze for a firmer texture.
6. Enjoy the delightful combination of warm, crispy churros and creamy vanilla ice cream in every bite!

B. Churros Bread Pudding with Bourbon Sauce
Ingredients for Churros Bread Pudding:

- Prepared churros from the previous recipe, cut into 1-inch pieces
- 4 cups stale bread cubes
- 4 large eggs
- 2 cups milk (dairy or non-dairy)
- 1/2 cup granulated sugar

- 1 teaspoon vanilla extract
- 1/2 teaspoon ground cinnamon
- Pinch of salt

Ingredients for Bourbon Sauce:

- 1/2 cup unsalted butter
- 1 cup granulated sugar
- 1/4 cup bourbon
- 1/4 cup heavy cream

Instructions for Churros Bread Pudding:

1. Preheat your oven to 350°F (175°C) and grease a baking dish.
2. In a large mixing bowl, whisk together the eggs, milk, sugar, vanilla extract, cinnamon, and salt.
3. Add the churros pieces and bread cubes to the egg mixture, stirring gently to combine and ensure all pieces are coated.
4. Pour the mixture into the prepared baking dish and let it sit for about 30 minutes, allowing the bread to absorb the liquid.
5. Bake in the preheated oven for 45-50 minutes, or until the top is golden brown and the pudding is set.
6. Remove from the oven and let it cool slightly before serving.

Instructions for Bourbon Sauce:

1. In a saucepan, melt the butter over medium heat.
2. Stir in the sugar and bourbon until the sugar is dissolved.
3. Bring the mixture to a simmer and cook for about 5 minutes, stirring occasionally.
4. Remove from heat and stir in the heavy cream.
5. Serve the warm churros bread pudding with a generous drizzle of bourbon sauce. Enjoy the comforting flavors of cinnamon, bourbon, and caramel!

C. Churros Trifle with Fresh Berries
Ingredients:

- Prepared churros from the previous recipe, cut into 1-inch pieces
- Fresh mixed berries (such as strawberries, blueberries, raspberries)
- Whipped cream or whipped coconut cream
- 1/4 cup chocolate shavings or cocoa powder (optional, for garnish)

Instructions:

1. In a trifle dish or individual serving glasses, layer the bottom with a portion of the prepared churros pieces.
2. Add a layer of fresh mixed berries on top of the churros.
3. Spread a layer of whipped cream or whipped coconut cream over the berries.
4. Repeat the layers until the trifle dish or glasses are filled, ending with a layer of whipped cream on top.
5. Garnish with chocolate shavings or a dusting of cocoa powder, if desired.
6. Refrigerate the churros trifle for at least 1 hour before serving to allow the flavors to meld together.
7. Serve chilled and enjoy the refreshing combination of crispy churros, sweet berries, and creamy whipped cream!

Chapter (6) Churros Candy Bar Inspired Beverages

A. Churros Milkshake with Whipped Cream and Sprinkles
Ingredients:

- 2 cups vanilla ice cream
- 1/2 cup milk (dairy or non-dairy)
- 2-3 prepared churros from the previous recipe
- Whipped cream
- Sprinkles

Instructions:

1. In a blender, combine vanilla ice cream, milk, and prepared churros broken into smaller pieces.
2. Blend until smooth and creamy.
3. Pour the churros milkshake into glasses.
4. Top each milkshake with a dollop of whipped cream and sprinkle with colorful sprinkles.
5. Serve immediately with a straw and enjoy the delightful sweetness of this churros-inspired treat!

B. Churros Hot Chocolate with Marshmallow Fluff
Ingredients:

- 2 cups milk (dairy or non-dairy)
- 1/4 cup cocoa powder
- 2-3 tablespoons granulated sugar (adjust to taste)
- 1/2 teaspoon ground cinnamon
- Prepared churros from the previous recipe
- Marshmallow fluff

Instructions:

1. In a saucepan, heat milk over medium heat until hot but not boiling.
2. Whisk in cocoa powder, sugar, and ground cinnamon until well combined and smooth.
3. Continue to heat the hot chocolate mixture, stirring frequently, until it reaches your desired temperature.
4. Pour the hot chocolate into mugs.
5. Top each mug with a swirl of marshmallow fluff.
6. Garnish with a whole churro or a churro stick for stirring.
7. Serve immediately and enjoy the cozy warmth of churros hot chocolate with fluffy marshmallow topping!

C. Churros Frappuccino with Caramel Swirl
Ingredients:

- 1 cup strong brewed coffee, cooled
- 1/2 cup milk (dairy or non-dairy)
- 2-3 prepared churros from the previous recipe
- 1 tablespoon caramel sauce
- Ice cubes
- Whipped cream (optional)
- Additional caramel sauce for drizzling (optional)

Instructions:

1. In a blender, combine cooled brewed coffee, milk, prepared churros broken into smaller pieces, and caramel sauce.
2. Add ice cubes to the blender until you reach your desired consistency.
3. Blend until smooth and creamy.

4. Pour the churros frappuccino into glasses.
5. Top with whipped cream if desired and drizzle with additional caramel sauce.
6. Serve immediately with a straw and enjoy the refreshing taste of this churros-inspired frappuccino!

Chapter (7) DIY Churros Candy Bar Party

A. Setting Up a Churros Candy Bar Station

Setting up a churros candy bar station is a fun and interactive way to entertain guests at your party. Here's how to do it:

1. Churros Making Station: Set up a table with all the ingredients and equipment needed to make churros. Include bowls of churro dough, piping bags, frying pans with oil, and toppings like cinnamon sugar, chocolate sauce, caramel sauce, and sprinkles.
2. Variety of Fillings: Offer a selection of fillings for stuffed churros, such as peanut butter, Nutella, fruit jams, and cream cheese.
3. Dipping Sauces: Provide an assortment of dipping sauces for guests to enjoy with their churros, including chocolate ganache, caramel sauce, fruit coulis, and whipped cream.
4. Decorative Plates and Napkins: Set out decorative plates, napkins, and utensils for guests to use when enjoying their churros creations.
5. Beverage Station: Offer a variety of beverages to accompany the churros, such as hot chocolate, coffee, flavored milk, and cold drinks.
6. Churros Display: Create an eye-catching display for the churros, using tiered stands, decorative trays, and serving platters to showcase the different varieties and toppings.
7. Instruction Cards: Provide instruction cards with step-by-step guides on how to make churros and suggestions for flavor combinations.
8. Personalization: Encourage guests to personalize their churros by adding their favorite toppings and fillings, and taking photos

of their creations to share on social media.

B. Churros Candy Bar Party Menu Ideas

For a complete churros candy bar party menu, consider including the following:

1. Savory Options: Offer savory churros variations, such as cheese-stuffed churros or churros served with savory dipping sauces like salsa or aioli, for guests who prefer a more savory treat.
2. Side Dishes: Accompany the churros with side dishes like fresh fruit platters, chips and salsa, or a selection of cheeses and crackers.
3. Desserts: In addition to churros, provide a variety of other desserts such as cookies, brownies, cupcakes, and fruit tarts to satisfy all tastes.
4. Beverages: Serve a range of beverages including hot and cold options such as coffee, tea, hot chocolate, flavored milk, fruit punch, and soft drinks.
5. DIY Activities: Consider incorporating DIY dessert activities like cookie decorating or cupcake decorating to add an extra element of fun to the party.

C. Churros Candy Bar Decoration and Presentation Tips

Theme: Choose a theme for your churros candy bar party, such as a fiesta theme with vibrant colors and festive decorations, or a rustic theme with natural textures and earthy tones.

1. Table Decor: Decorate the churros candy bar station with colorful tablecloths, bunting, and banners featuring churros and candy bar motifs.
2. Centerpieces: Create eye-catching centerpieces using arrangements of fresh flowers, fruit, or decorative items that tie in with the party theme.

3. Signage: Use chalkboard signs or printed banners to label different stations and menu items, and to provide instructions and information for guests.

4. Lighting: Set the mood with ambient lighting such as fairy lights, candles, or lanterns to create a warm and inviting atmosphere.

5. Presentation: Arrange churros and toppings in attractive displays, using tiered stands, glass jars, and serving trays to showcase them effectively.

6. Personalization: Add personal touches such as custom labels, tags, or flags with guests' names or messages to make the churros candy bar party feel extra special.

With these tips, you can create a memorable churros candy bar party that your guests will love!

Chapter (8) Churros Candy Bar Around the World

A. Mexican Churros with Cajeta

Ingredients:

- Prepared churros from the previous recipe
- Cajeta (Mexican caramel sauce)
- Chopped nuts (optional, for garnish)

Instructions:

1. Prepare the churros according to the recipe instructions from the previous section.
2. Warm the cajeta in a saucepan over low heat or in the microwave until it's pourable.
3. Dip the warm churros into the cajeta sauce, coating them generously.
4. Optional: Sprinkle chopped nuts over the cajeta-coated churros for added crunch and flavor.
5. Serve the Mexican churros with cajeta immediately and enjoy the rich, caramel goodness!

B. Spanish Chocolate-Dipped Churros

Ingredients:

- Prepared churros from the previous recipe
- 1/2 cup dark chocolate chips
- 1/4 cup heavy cream
- 1 tablespoon unsalted butter
- Pinch of sea salt

Instructions:

1. Prepare the churros according to the recipe instructions from the previous section.
2. In a microwave-safe bowl, combine dark chocolate chips, heavy cream, butter, and a pinch of sea salt.
3. Microwave the chocolate mixture in 30-second intervals, stirring each time, until the chocolate is melted and smooth.
4. Dip the warm churros into the melted chocolate, coating them halfway or fully as desired.
5. Place the chocolate-dipped churros on a wire rack or parchment paper-lined tray to set.
6. Serve the Spanish churros with chocolate dipping sauce immediately, and savor the indulgent combination of crispy dough and rich chocolate!

C. Filipino Churros with Tsokolate
Ingredients for Tsokolate:

- 2 cups water
- 4 tablespoons tablea (Filipino cocoa tablets) or unsweetened cocoa powder
- 1/4 cup granulated sugar (adjust to taste)
- Pinch of salt
- Evaporated milk or coconut milk (optional, for serving)

Instructions for Tsokolate:

1. In a saucepan, combine water, tablea or cocoa powder, sugar, and a pinch of salt.
2. Bring the mixture to a simmer over medium heat, stirring constantly until the tablea or cocoa powder is dissolved and the mixture is smooth.
3. Adjust the sweetness according to your preference by adding

more sugar if needed.

4. Serve the tsokolate hot in individual cups or mugs.
5. Optionally, offer evaporated milk or coconut milk on the side for guests to customize their tsokolate.

Chapter (9) Churros Candy Bar Baking Techniques

A. Mastering the Art of Piping Perfect Churros

Piping churros may seem daunting, but with the right technique, you can achieve beautifully shaped churros every time:

1. Use the Right Piping Tip: A star-shaped piping tip is traditionally used for churros, as it creates the signature ridges and texture. Use a large open star tip for thicker churros and a smaller tip for thinner ones.
2. Maintain Consistent Pressure: Apply even pressure to the piping bag as you squeeze out the dough. This helps ensure that the churros are uniform in size and shape.
3. Pipe Smoothly: Hold the piping bag at a 45-degree angle above the oil, and steadily pipe the dough in a straight line. Use a pair of kitchen scissors to cut the dough cleanly from the piping tip to achieve neat ends.
4. Practice Makes Perfect: If you're new to piping churros, practice on a sheet of parchment paper before frying. This allows you to get a feel for the pressure and movement required to pipe smooth and consistent churros.

B. Achieving the Ideal Crunch: Frying Tips and Tricks

Frying churros to perfection requires attention to detail and the right frying techniques:

1. Maintain the Right Temperature: Heat the oil to the correct temperature (usually around 350°F/175°C) before frying. Use a candy thermometer to monitor the oil temperature and adjust the heat as needed to keep it consistent.
2. Don't Crowd the Pan: Fry the churros in small batches to avoid

overcrowding the pan, which can lower the oil temperature and result in soggy churros. Give them enough space to fry evenly and develop a crispy exterior.

3. Flip Them Halfway: To ensure even frying, flip the churros halfway through the cooking time using tongs or a slotted spoon. This helps them achieve a uniform golden brown color and crispy texture on all sides.

4. Drain Excess Oil: Once fried, transfer the churros to a paper towel-lined plate to drain excess oil. This helps prevent them from becoming greasy and maintains their crispiness.

C. Secrets to Creating Irresistibly Fluffy Churros

While churros are known for their crispy exterior, they should also have a light and fluffy interior. Here's how to achieve that perfect balance:

1. Use the Right Dough Consistency: The churro dough should be thick and sturdy enough to hold its shape when piped but still soft and pliable. Avoid adding too much flour, as this can result in dense and heavy churros.

2. Incorporate Air into the Dough: Whip the dough thoroughly to incorporate air, which helps create a lighter texture. Mix the dough until it becomes smooth and slightly elastic, with no lumps remaining.

3. Let the Dough Rest: Allow the churro dough to rest for at least 10-15 minutes before piping and frying. This allows the gluten to relax, resulting in a softer and fluffier texture once cooked.

4. Choose the Right Oil: Use a neutral-flavored oil with a high smoke point, such as vegetable oil or canola oil, for frying churros. This helps maintain the integrity of the dough and prevents it from absorbing too much oil, resulting in lighter and fluffier churros.

With these baking techniques, you'll be well on your way to mastering the art of churro-making and creating irresistible churros that are crispy on the outside and fluffy on the inside. Happy baking!

Chapter (10) Churros Candy Bar Flavor Infusions

A. Lavender Honey Churros with Lavender Sugar
Ingredients for Lavender Sugar:

- 1/4 cup granulated sugar
- 1 tablespoon culinary lavender buds

Ingredients for Lavender Honey Churros:

- Prepared churros dough from the previous recipe
- Honey
- Vegetable oil, for frying

Instructions for Lavender Sugar:

1. In a spice grinder or mortar and pestle, combine granulated sugar and culinary lavender buds.
2. Grind or crush the mixture until the lavender is finely ground and evenly distributed throughout the sugar.

Instructions for Lavender Honey Churros:

1. Prepare the churros dough according to the recipe instructions from the previous section.
2. Heat vegetable oil in a deep skillet or pot over medium-high heat until it reaches 350°F (175°C).
3. Carefully pipe the churro dough into the hot oil, forming traditional churros.
4. Fry the churros until golden brown and crispy, then transfer them to a paper towel-lined plate to drain excess oil.
5. While the churros are still warm, drizzle them generously with

honey.

6. Sprinkle the lavender sugar over the honey-drizzled churros, coating them evenly.
7. Serve the lavender honey churros immediately and enjoy the delicate floral flavor with a hint of sweetness!

B. Espresso Churros with Mocha Dipping Sauce
Ingredients for Mocha Dipping Sauce:

- 1/2 cup heavy cream
- 1/4 cup dark chocolate chips
- 1 tablespoon espresso powder
- 1 tablespoon granulated sugar (optional, for sweetness)

Ingredients for Espresso Churros:

- Prepared churros dough from the previous recipe
- 1 tablespoon espresso powder
- Vegetable oil, for frying

Instructions for Mocha Dipping Sauce:

1. In a saucepan, heat the heavy cream over medium heat until it begins to simmer.
2. Remove from heat and stir in the dark chocolate chips and espresso powder until the chocolate is melted and smooth.
3. Taste and add granulated sugar if desired for sweetness.
4. Transfer the mocha dipping sauce to a serving bowl and set aside.

Instructions for Espresso Churros:

1. Prepare the churros dough according to the recipe instructions from the previous section, adding espresso powder to the dough

for flavor.

2. Heat vegetable oil in a deep skillet or pot over medium-high heat until it reaches 350°F (175°C).
3. Carefully pipe the espresso-infused churro dough into the hot oil, forming traditional churros.
4. Fry the churros until golden brown and crispy, then transfer them to a paper towel-lined plate to drain excess oil.
5. Serve the espresso churros with the mocha dipping sauce on the side for dipping, and enjoy the rich coffee flavor with a hint of chocolate!

C. Orange Zest and Dark Chocolate Churros
Ingredients for Orange Zest Sugar:

- 1/4 cup granulated sugar
- Zest of 1 orange

Ingredients for Orange Zest and Dark Chocolate Churros:

- Prepared churros dough from the previous recipe
- Zest of 1 orange
- Dark chocolate for melting
- Vegetable oil, for frying

Instructions for Orange Zest Sugar:

1. In a bowl, combine granulated sugar and the zest of one orange.
2. Mix well until the orange zest is evenly distributed throughout the sugar.

Instructions for Orange Zest and Dark Chocolate Churros:

1. Prepare the churros dough according to the recipe instructions from the previous section.

2. Heat vegetable oil in a deep skillet or pot over medium-high heat until it reaches 350°F (175°C).

3. Carefully pipe the churro dough into the hot oil, forming traditional churros.

4. Fry the churros until golden brown and crispy, then transfer them to a paper towel-lined plate to drain excess oil.

5. While the churros are still warm, sprinkle them with the orange zest sugar, coating them evenly.

6. Melt the dark chocolate in a microwave-safe bowl in 30-second intervals, stirring until smooth.

7. Drizzle the melted chocolate over the orange zest-coated churros.

8. Serve the orange zest and dark chocolate churros immediately and enjoy the refreshing citrus flavor combined with rich chocolate decadence!

Chapter (11) Churros Candy Bar Breakfast Delights

A. Churros French Toast Sticks with Maple Syrup
Ingredients:

- Prepared churros from the previous recipe
- 4 slices of thick-cut bread, preferably brioche or challah
- 2 large eggs
- 1/4 cup milk
- 1 teaspoon vanilla extract
- 1/2 teaspoon ground cinnamon
- Butter, for frying
- Maple syrup, for serving

Instructions:

1. Cut the prepared churros into smaller pieces to resemble French toast sticks.
2. In a shallow dish, whisk together eggs, milk, vanilla extract, and ground cinnamon to make the French toast batter.
3. Heat a skillet or griddle over medium heat and melt a knob of butter.
4. Dip each churros stick into the egg mixture, coating it evenly, then place it in the skillet.
5. Cook the churros French toast sticks for 2-3 minutes on each side, or until golden brown and crispy.
6. Remove from the skillet and serve hot with maple syrup for dipping or drizzling.

B. Churros Waffles with Whipped Cream and Berries

Ingredients:

- Prepared churros from the previous recipe
- Waffle batter (prepared according to your favorite recipe or using a boxed mix)
- Whipped cream
- Fresh berries (such as strawberries, blueberries, raspberries)

Instructions:

1. Preheat your waffle iron according to the manufacturer's instructions.
2. Cut the prepared churros into smaller pieces to fit into the waffle iron.
3. Place the churros pieces onto the preheated waffle iron and pour the waffle batter over them.
4. Close the waffle iron and cook the churros waffles according to the manufacturer's instructions, until they are golden brown and crispy.
5. Carefully remove the churros waffles from the waffle iron and transfer them to serving plates.
6. Top the churros waffles with a dollop of whipped cream and a generous serving of fresh berries.
7. Serve immediately and enjoy the delightful combination of crispy churros and fluffy waffles with sweet whipped cream and berries.

C. Churros Pancakes with Chocolate Hazelnut Spread
Ingredients:

- Prepared churros from the previous recipe
- Pancake batter (prepared according to your favorite recipe or using a boxed mix)
- Chocolate hazelnut spread (such as Nutella)

Instructions:

1. Cut the prepared churros into smaller pieces to mix into the pancake batter.
2. Prepare the pancake batter according to the recipe or package instructions.
3. Gently fold the churros pieces into the pancake batter until evenly distributed.
4. Heat a skillet or griddle over medium heat and lightly grease with butter or oil.
5. Pour the pancake batter onto the skillet to form pancakes of your desired size.
6. Cook the churros pancakes for 2-3 minutes on each side, or until golden brown and cooked through.
7. Remove the pancakes from the skillet and spread a layer of chocolate hazelnut spread between each pancake.
8. Serve the churros pancakes stacked high and drizzle with additional chocolate hazelnut spread if desired.
9. Enjoy the indulgent combination of fluffy pancakes and crispy churros with rich chocolate hazelnut spread!

Chapter (12) Churros Candy Bar for Special Occasions

A. Churros Wedding Cake Tower

For a unique and memorable wedding dessert, consider a churros wedding cake tower:

1. Churros Preparation: Prepare a large quantity of churros in various shapes and sizes, including traditional sticks, loops, and spirals. Customize the churros with different coatings and fillings to suit the wedding theme and preferences of the couple.

2. Tiered Display: Arrange the churros on tiered cake stands or towers to create a stunning display. Start with a wide base of churros and stack them upwards in a pyramid shape, with the smallest churros at the top.

3. Decorations: Decorate the churros wedding cake tower with fresh flowers, greenery, and decorative elements that match the wedding theme and color scheme. Add personalized touches such as cake toppers, banners, or signage to celebrate the couple's special day.

4. Dipping Sauces: Provide a variety of dipping sauces for guests to enjoy with their churros, such as chocolate ganache, caramel sauce, fruit coulis, and whipped cream. Display the sauces in elegant bowls or jars around the base of the churros tower for easy access.

5. Wedding Cake Cutting Ceremony: Instead of a traditional cake cutting ceremony, invite the newlyweds to share a special moment by cutting into the churros wedding cake tower together. Guests can then enjoy the delicious churros as a sweet finale to the celebration.

B. Churros Candy Bar Birthday Party Ideas

Celebrate a birthday in style with a churros candy bar party:

1. Churros Station: Set up a churros candy bar station with various types of churros, dipping sauces, and toppings for guests to customize their treats. Include options like classic churros, filled churros, and churro bites for variety.

2. Themed Decorations: Decorate the party space with colorful banners, balloons, and signage featuring churros and candy bar motifs. Set the mood with festive music and lighting to create a fun and lively atmosphere.

3. Party Activities: Plan interactive activities such as churros decorating contests, churro-eating competitions, or DIY churros making stations where guests can try their hand at piping and frying churros.

4. Birthday Cake Alternative: Instead of a traditional birthday cake, consider a churros cake or tower as the centerpiece dessert. Customize the churros with birthday-themed decorations, sprinkles, and candles for a festive touch.

5. Party Favors: Send guests home with delicious party favors such as mini bags of churros, churro-flavored snacks, or homemade churros kits so they can continue the celebration at home.

C. Churros Candy Bar Holiday Treats

Add a festive twist to your holiday celebrations with churros candy bar treats:

1. Holiday Churros: Create holiday-themed churros by incorporating seasonal flavors and decorations. For example, dust churros with cinnamon sugar and edible gold glitter for a festive touch, or fill them with pumpkin spice cream for Thanksgiving.

2. Holiday Dipping Sauces: Offer holiday-inspired dipping sauces

such as cranberry compote, peppermint chocolate ganache, or gingerbread caramel for guests to enjoy with their churros.

3. Holiday Churros Cocktails: Serve up festive churros cocktails featuring holiday flavors like eggnog, spiced cider, or mulled wine. Pair these drinks with churros sticks for a delicious and festive treat.

4. Churros Gift Boxes: Package homemade churros in festive gift boxes or bags to give as holiday gifts to friends and family. Include a variety of churros flavors and dipping sauces for an extra special treat.

5. Churros Dessert Buffet: Create a holiday-themed churros dessert buffet with an assortment of churros, cakes, cookies, and candies. Decorate the buffet table with holiday decorations, lights, and greenery for a festive display.

With these ideas, you can make any special occasion even more memorable with a delightful churros candy bar experience!

Chapter (13) Churros Candy Bar Savory Creations

A. Churros-Crusted Chicken Tenders with Spicy Dipping Sauce
Ingredients for Churros-Crusted Chicken Tenders:

- 1 lb chicken tenders
- Salt and pepper, to taste
- 1 cup all-purpose flour
- 2 eggs, beaten
- 1 cup breadcrumbs
- 1 cup crushed churros
- Vegetable oil, for frying

Ingredients for Spicy Dipping Sauce:

- 1/2 cup mayonnaise
- 2 tablespoons hot sauce
- 1 tablespoon honey
- 1 teaspoon paprika
- 1/2 teaspoon garlic powder
- Salt and pepper, to taste

Instructions:

1. Season the chicken tenders with salt and pepper.
2. Set up a breading station with three shallow dishes: one with flour, one with beaten eggs, and one with a mixture of breadcrumbs and crushed churros.
3. Dredge each chicken tender in the flour, then dip into the beaten eggs, and finally coat with the churro breadcrumb mixture, pressing gently to adhere.
4. Heat vegetable oil in a skillet over medium-high heat.

5. Fry the churros-crusted chicken tenders in the hot oil for 3-4 minutes per side, or until golden brown and cooked through.
6. Remove the chicken tenders from the oil and drain on a paper towel-lined plate.
7. In a small bowl, whisk together the ingredients for the spicy dipping sauce until smooth and well combined.
8. Serve the churros-crusted chicken tenders hot with the spicy dipping sauce on the side.

B. Churros-Stuffed Jalapeños with Cream Cheese
Ingredients:

- 12 large jalapeños
- 4 ounces cream cheese, softened
- Crushed churros
- Bacon slices, cut into halves
- Toothpicks

Instructions:

1. Preheat the oven to 375°F (190°C) and line a baking sheet with parchment paper.
2. Cut the jalapeños in half lengthwise and remove the seeds and membranes.
3. Fill each jalapeño half with softened cream cheese.
4. Sprinkle crushed churros over the cream cheese-filled jalapeños.
5. Wrap each jalapeño half with a bacon slice and secure with a toothpick.
6. Place the stuffed jalapeños on the prepared baking sheet.
7. Bake in the preheated oven for 20-25 minutes, or until the bacon is crispy and the jalapeños are tender.
8. Serve the churros-stuffed jalapeños hot as a savory appetizer or snack.

C. Churros Pizza with Caramelized Onions and Bacon
Ingredients for Churros Pizza Dough:

- 1 packet (2 1/4 teaspoons) active dry yeast
- 1 cup warm water
- 2 1/2 cups all-purpose flour
- 1 tablespoon sugar
- 1 teaspoon salt
- 2 tablespoons olive oil

Additional Ingredients:

- Caramelized onions
- Cooked bacon, chopped
- Shredded mozzarella cheese
- Crushed churros

Instructions:

1. In a small bowl, dissolve the yeast in warm water and let it sit for 5 minutes until frothy.
2. In a large mixing bowl, combine the flour, sugar, and salt.
3. Add the yeast mixture and olive oil to the flour mixture and stir until a dough forms.
4. Knead the dough on a floured surface for 5-7 minutes until smooth and elastic.
5. Place the dough in a greased bowl, cover with a clean kitchen towel, and let it rise in a warm place for 1-2 hours, or until doubled in size.
6. Preheat the oven to 425°F (220°C) and lightly grease a pizza pan or baking sheet.
7. Roll out the risen dough on a floured surface to your desired thickness.
8. Transfer the rolled-out dough to the prepared pizza pan.

9. Top the pizza dough with caramelized onions, chopped bacon, and shredded mozzarella cheese.
10. Sprinkle crushed churros over the pizza toppings.
11. Bake in the preheated oven for 15-20 minutes, or until the crust is golden brown and the cheese is melted and bubbly.
12. Slice the churros pizza and serve hot as a savory twist on a classic favorite.

Chapter (14) Churros Candy Bar for Kids

A. Churros Candy Bar Making Parties for Children

Hosting a churros candy bar making party for children is a fun and interactive way to celebrate special occasions or just enjoy a tasty treat together. Here's how to organize the perfect churros candy bar party:

1. Invitations: Send out colorful invitations to the guests, inviting them to a churros candy bar making party. Include fun details about the event, such as the date, time, location, and any special instructions.

2. Churros Station: Set up a churros making station with all the necessary ingredients and equipment. Provide pre-made churros dough, piping bags, frying pans, cooking oil, and a variety of toppings and dipping sauces for the children to choose from.

3. Decorations: Decorate the party space with colorful banners, balloons, and tablecloths featuring churros and candy bar motifs. Create a festive atmosphere with music and party games to keep the children entertained.

4. Churros Making: Let the children get creative by piping and frying their own churros. Supervise them closely to ensure safety and help them with any tricky steps. Encourage them to experiment with different shapes, sizes, and toppings to make their churros unique.

5. Tasting and Sharing: Once the churros are cooked, invite the children to taste their creations and share them with their friends. Provide plenty of napkins and plates for easy serving and cleanup.

6. Crafts and Activities: Keep the children entertained with churros-themed crafts and activities, such as decorating churros-shaped cookies, making churros-inspired artwork, or playing

pin the churro on the donkey.

7. Party Favors: Send the children home with sweet memories and a churros-themed party favor, such as mini bags of churros, homemade churros kits, or churros-shaped cookies decorated by the children themselves.

B. Churros Candy Bar Lunchbox Ideas

Make lunchtime extra special with churros candy bar-inspired lunchbox ideas that kids will love:

1. Churros Sticks: Pack mini churros sticks in the lunchbox for a tasty snack. Pair them with a small container of chocolate or caramel dipping sauce for dipping.
2. Churros Sandwiches: Use churros as the bread for a fun and creative sandwich. Spread peanut butter and jelly between two churros sticks for a sweet and savory treat.
3. Churros Bites: Pack bite-sized churros in the lunchbox for easy snacking. Sprinkle them with cinnamon sugar or powdered sugar for extra flavor.
4. Churros Muffins: Bake churros-flavored muffins for a delicious and portable lunchbox option. Add chocolate chips or diced apples to the muffin batter for added sweetness.
5. Churros Fruit Skewers: Thread chunks of fresh fruit onto skewers alternating with mini churros for a colorful and nutritious snack.
6. Churros Yogurt Parfait: Layer vanilla yogurt with crushed churros and sliced bananas or berries in a small container for a tasty and satisfying dessert.

C. Churros Candy Bar Inspired Crafts and Activities

Keep kids entertained and engaged with churros candy bar-inspired crafts and activities:

1. Churros Art: Provide children with paper, markers, and glitter to create their own churros-inspired artwork. Encourage them to draw colorful churros shapes and decorate them with sprinkles and frosting.
2. Churros Necklace Making: Set up a craft station with churros-shaped beads and colorful string for children to make their own churros necklaces. They can wear their creations proudly or give them as gifts to friends and family.
3. Churros Tasting Challenge: Blindfold the children and have them taste different types of churros to guess the flavors. Award prizes to the children who correctly identify the most flavors.
4. Churros Story Time: Read children's books about churros or candy bars and discuss the themes and characters together. Encourage children to use their imagination to create their own churros-themed stories or drawings.
5. Churros Dance Party: Play upbeat music and encourage children to dance and move their bodies like churros. Have a dance-off or follow-along dance routines for extra fun and laughter.

With these churros candy bar-inspired ideas, children can enjoy delicious treats, engage in creative activities, and make lasting memories with their friends and family.

Chapter (15) Churros Candy Bar Fusion Desserts

A. Churros Tiramisu with Coffee Soaked Ladyfingers
Ingredients:
For the Churros:

- Prepared churros dough from the previous recipe
- Vegetable oil, for frying
- 1/2 cup granulated sugar
- 1 tablespoon ground cinnamon

For the Tiramisu:

- 1 cup strong brewed coffee, cooled
- 2 tablespoons coffee liqueur (optional)
- 1 cup heavy cream
- 1 cup mascarpone cheese
- 1/4 cup powdered sugar
- Cocoa powder, for dusting

Instructions:

1. Prepare the churros dough according to the recipe instructions from the previous section.
2. Heat vegetable oil in a deep skillet or pot over medium-high heat until it reaches 350°F (175°C).
3. Carefully pipe the churro dough into the hot oil, forming traditional churros.
4. Fry the churros until golden brown and crispy, then transfer them to a paper towel-lined plate to drain excess oil.
5. In a shallow dish, mix together the granulated sugar and ground cinnamon. Roll the fried churros in the cinnamon sugar

mixture until evenly coated. Set aside.

6. In a mixing bowl, whip the heavy cream until stiff peaks form. In another bowl, beat the mascarpone cheese and powdered sugar until smooth. Fold the whipped cream into the mascarpone mixture until well combined.

7. In a shallow dish, combine the cooled brewed coffee and coffee liqueur (if using). Quickly dip ladyfinger biscuits into the coffee mixture, ensuring they are soaked but not soggy.

8. Arrange a layer of soaked ladyfingers in the bottom of a serving dish or individual dessert glasses.

9. Spread a layer of the mascarpone cream mixture over the soaked ladyfingers.

10. Arrange a layer of cinnamon sugar-coated churros over the mascarpone cream layer.

11. Repeat the layers of soaked ladyfingers, mascarpone cream, and churros until the serving dish is filled, ending with a layer of mascarpone cream on top.

12. Cover and refrigerate the churros tiramisu for at least 4 hours, or overnight, to allow the flavors to meld.

13. Before serving, dust the top of the tiramisu with cocoa powder for garnish.

14. Serve chilled and enjoy the delightful fusion of churros and tiramisu flavors!

B. Churros Baklava with Honey Nut Filling
Ingredients:
For the Churros:

- Prepared churros dough from the previous recipe
- Vegetable oil, for frying
- 1/2 cup granulated sugar
- 1 tablespoon ground cinnamon

For the Honey Nut Filling:

- 1 cup mixed nuts (such as walnuts, almonds, and pistachios), finely chopped
- 1/2 cup honey
- 1 teaspoon ground cinnamon

For the Syrup:

- 1/2 cup honey
- 1/2 cup water
- 1/2 cup granulated sugar
- 1 cinnamon stick
- 1 teaspoon lemon juice

Instructions:

1. Prepare the churros dough according to the recipe instructions from the previous section.
2. Heat vegetable oil in a deep skillet or pot over medium-high heat until it reaches 350°F (175°C).
3. Carefully pipe the churro dough into the hot oil, forming traditional churros.
4. Fry the churros until golden brown and crispy, then transfer them to a paper towel-lined plate to drain excess oil.
5. In a shallow dish, mix together the granulated sugar and ground cinnamon. Roll the fried churros in the cinnamon sugar mixture until evenly coated. Set aside.
6. In a mixing bowl, combine the finely chopped mixed nuts, honey, and ground cinnamon to make the honey nut filling.
7. Prepare the syrup by combining honey, water, granulated sugar, cinnamon stick, and lemon juice in a saucepan. Bring to a simmer over medium heat, stirring until the sugar is dissolved. Reduce the heat to low and simmer for 5 minutes. Remove from

heat and let the syrup cool slightly.

8. Preheat the oven to 350°F (175°C). Grease a baking dish with butter.

9. Arrange a layer of cinnamon sugar-coated churros in the bottom of the greased baking dish.

10. Spread a layer of the honey nut filling over the churros layer.

11. Repeat the layers of churros and honey nut filling until the baking dish is filled, ending with a layer of churros on top.

12. Pour the cooled syrup over the assembled churros baklava, ensuring it is evenly distributed.

13. Bake in the preheated oven for 20-25 minutes, or until the churros are golden brown and crispy.

14. Remove from the oven and let the churros baklava cool slightly before serving.

15. Serve warm or at room temperature, and enjoy the delicious fusion of churros and baklava flavors!

C. Churros Cannoli with Ricotta Cream and Chocolate Chips
Ingredients:
For the Churros:

- Prepared churros dough from the previous recipe
- Vegetable oil, for frying
- 1/2 cup granulated sugar
- 1 tablespoon ground cinnamon

For the Ricotta Cream Filling:

- 1 cup ricotta cheese
- 1/2 cup powdered sugar
- 1 teaspoon vanilla extract
- 1/4 cup mini chocolate chips

Instructions:

1. Prepare the churros dough according to the recipe instructions from the previous section.
2. Heat vegetable oil in a deep skillet or pot over medium-high heat until it reaches 350°F (175°C).
3. Carefully pipe the churro dough into the hot oil, forming traditional churros.
4. Fry the churros until golden brown and crispy, then transfer them to a paper towel-lined plate to drain excess oil.
5. In a shallow dish, mix together the granulated sugar and ground cinnamon. Roll the fried churros in the cinnamon sugar mixture until evenly coated. Set aside.
6. In a mixing bowl, combine the ricotta cheese, powdered sugar, and vanilla extract to make the ricotta cream filling. Stir in the mini chocolate chips.
7. Using a piping bag or a small spoon, fill the cooled churros with the ricotta cream filling.
8. Arrange the filled churros on a serving platter or individual plates.
9. Serve the churros cannoli immediately and enjoy the delightful fusion of churros and cannoli flavors!

Chapter (16) Churros Candy Bar International Influences

A. Japanese Matcha Churros with Red Bean Paste
Ingredients:
For the Matcha Churros:

- Prepared churros dough from the previous recipe
- 1 tablespoon matcha powder
- Vegetable oil, for frying
- 1/2 cup granulated sugar
- 1 tablespoon matcha powder (for dusting)

For the Red Bean Paste:

- 1 cup cooked red beans (adzuki beans)
- 1/2 cup granulated sugar
- 2 tablespoons water

Instructions:

1. Prepare the churros dough according to the recipe instructions from the previous section.
2. In a small bowl, mix 1 tablespoon of matcha powder into the churros dough until well combined.
3. Heat vegetable oil in a deep skillet or pot over medium-high heat until it reaches 350°F (175°C).
4. Carefully pipe the matcha churro dough into the hot oil, forming traditional churros.
5. Fry the matcha churros until golden brown and crispy, then transfer them to a paper towel-lined plate to drain excess oil.
6. In a shallow dish, mix together the granulated sugar and 1 tablespoon of matcha powder. Roll the fried matcha churros in

the matcha sugar mixture until evenly coated. Set aside.

7. To make the red bean paste, combine cooked red beans, granulated sugar, and water in a saucepan. Cook over medium heat, stirring occasionally, until the mixture thickens into a paste-like consistency. Remove from heat and let it cool slightly.

8. Using a piping bag or a small spoon, fill the cooled matcha churros with the red bean paste filling.

9. Arrange the filled matcha churros on a serving platter or individual plates.

10. Serve the Japanese matcha churros with red bean paste immediately and enjoy the delightful fusion of flavors!

B. Indian Spiced Churros with Cardamom Sugar
Ingredients:
For the Spiced Churros:

- Prepared churros dough from the previous recipe
- 1 teaspoon ground cardamom
- 1/2 teaspoon ground cinnamon
- 1/4 teaspoon ground ginger
- Vegetable oil, for frying

For the Cardamom Sugar:

- 1/2 cup granulated sugar
- 1 teaspoon ground cardamom

Instructions:

1. Prepare the churros dough according to the recipe instructions from the previous section.

2. In a small bowl, mix ground cardamom, ground cinnamon, and

ground ginger into the churros dough until well combined.

3. Heat vegetable oil in a deep skillet or pot over medium-high heat until it reaches 350°F (175°C).

4. Carefully pipe the spiced churro dough into the hot oil, forming traditional churros.

5. Fry the spiced churros until golden brown and crispy, then transfer them to a paper towel-lined plate to drain excess oil.

6. In a shallow dish, mix together the granulated sugar and ground cardamom. Roll the fried spiced churros in the cardamom sugar mixture until evenly coated. Set aside.

7. Arrange the spiced churros on a serving platter or individual plates.

8. Serve the Indian spiced churros with cardamom sugar immediately and enjoy the delightful fusion of flavors!

C. Italian Cannoli-Stuffed Churros with Pistachios
Ingredients:
For the Churros:

- Prepared churros dough from the previous recipe
- Vegetable oil, for frying
- 1/2 cup granulated sugar
- 1 teaspoon ground cinnamon

For the Cannoli Filling:

- 1 cup ricotta cheese
- 1/4 cup powdered sugar
- 1/4 teaspoon vanilla extract
- 1/4 cup mini chocolate chips
- 1/4 cup chopped pistachios

Instructions:

1. Prepare the churros dough according to the recipe instructions from the previous section.
2. Heat vegetable oil in a deep skillet or pot over medium-high heat until it reaches 350°F (175°C).
3. Carefully pipe the churro dough into the hot oil, forming traditional churros.
4. Fry the churros until golden brown and crispy, then transfer them to a paper towel-lined plate to drain excess oil.
5. In a shallow dish, mix together the granulated sugar and ground cinnamon. Roll the fried churros in the cinnamon sugar mixture until evenly coated. Set aside.
6. In a mixing bowl, combine ricotta cheese, powdered sugar, and vanilla extract to make the cannoli filling. Stir in mini chocolate chips and chopped pistachios.
7. Using a piping bag or a small spoon, fill the cooled churros with the cannoli filling.
8. Arrange the filled churros on a serving platter or individual plates.
9. Serve the Italian cannoli-stuffed churros immediately and enjoy the delightful fusion of flavors!

Chapter (17) Churros Candy Bar Healthier Alternatives

A. Baked Churros with Reduced Sugar Options
Ingredients:
For the Baked Churros:

- 1 cup water
- 2 tablespoons vegetable oil
- 2 tablespoons granulated sugar (or sweetener of choice)
- 1/2 teaspoon salt
- 1 cup all-purpose flour
- 2 eggs
- 1/2 teaspoon vanilla extract
- Cooking spray

For the Reduced Sugar Options:

- Stevia or monk fruit sweetener instead of granulated sugar
- Sugar-free chocolate for dipping
- Sugar-free caramel sauce for drizzling

Instructions:

1. Preheat the oven to 400°F (200°C) and line a baking sheet with parchment paper. Lightly coat the parchment paper with cooking spray.
2. In a saucepan, combine water, vegetable oil, sugar (or sweetener), and salt. Bring to a boil over medium heat.
3. Remove the saucepan from the heat and stir in the flour until the mixture forms a dough.
4. Add the eggs one at a time, mixing well after each addition. Stir in the vanilla extract.

5. Transfer the churro dough to a piping bag fitted with a star tip.
6. Pipe the dough onto the prepared baking sheet, forming churros of desired length.
7. Bake in the preheated oven for 20-25 minutes, or until the churros are golden brown and crispy.
8. While the churros are baking, prepare the reduced sugar options by using stevia or monk fruit sweetener in place of granulated sugar, and opting for sugar-free chocolate and caramel sauce for dipping and drizzling.
9. Remove the baked churros from the oven and let them cool slightly before serving with the reduced sugar options.

B. Air-Fried Churros with Lighter Dipping Sauces
Ingredients:
For the Air-Fried Churros:

- Prepared churros dough from the previous recipe
- Cooking spray

For the Lighter Dipping Sauces:

- Greek yogurt mixed with honey or agave syrup for a creamy dip
- Fresh fruit puree (such as raspberry or mango) for a naturally sweet option
- Unsweetened applesauce flavored with cinnamon for a low-calorie alternative

Instructions:

1. Preheat the air fryer to 375°F (190°C).
2. Lightly coat the air fryer basket with cooking spray.
3. Transfer the prepared churro dough to a piping bag fitted with a star tip.
4. Pipe the dough into the air fryer basket, forming churros of

desired length, leaving space between each churro.

5. Air fry the churros in batches for 8-10 minutes, or until golden brown and crispy.

6. While the churros are cooking, prepare the lighter dipping sauces by mixing Greek yogurt with honey or agave syrup, preparing fresh fruit purees, or flavoring unsweetened applesauce with cinnamon.

7. Remove the air-fried churros from the air fryer and let them cool slightly before serving with the lighter dipping sauces.

C. Whole Wheat Churros with Fruit Compote

Ingredients:

For the Whole Wheat Churros:

- 1 cup water
- 2 tablespoons vegetable oil
- 2 tablespoons honey or maple syrup
- 1/2 teaspoon salt
- 1 cup whole wheat flour
- 2 eggs
- 1/2 teaspoon vanilla extract
- Cooking spray

For the Fruit Compote:

- 2 cups mixed fresh or frozen fruits (such as berries, peaches, or apples)
- 2 tablespoons honey or maple syrup
- 1 teaspoon lemon juice
- 1/2 teaspoon ground cinnamon

Instructions:

1. In a saucepan, combine water, vegetable oil, honey or maple

syrup, and salt. Bring to a boil over medium heat.

2. Remove the saucepan from the heat and stir in the whole wheat flour until the mixture forms a dough.

3. Add the eggs one at a time, mixing well after each addition. Stir in the vanilla extract.

4. Transfer the churro dough to a piping bag fitted with a star tip.

5. Preheat the oven to 400°F (200°C) and line a baking sheet with parchment paper. Lightly coat the parchment paper with cooking spray.

6. Pipe the dough onto the prepared baking sheet, forming churros of desired length.

7. Bake in the preheated oven for 20-25 minutes, or until the churros are golden brown and crispy.

8. While the churros are baking, prepare the fruit compote by combining mixed fruits, honey or maple syrup, lemon juice, and ground cinnamon in a saucepan. Cook over medium heat, stirring occasionally, until the fruits are soft and the mixture thickens into a compote.

9. Remove the baked whole wheat churros from the oven and let them cool slightly before serving with the fruit compote.

Chapter (18) Churros Candy Bar Pairing Suggestions

A. Wine and Churros: Perfect Pairings

Churros, with their crispy exterior and soft interior, pair wonderfully with a variety of wines. Here are some perfect wine and churros pairings to elevate your indulgent experience:

1. Sweet Moscato: The light, effervescent nature of sweet Moscato complements the cinnamon sugar coating of churros, enhancing their sweetness without overpowering the palate.
2. Late Harvest Riesling: The rich, honeyed flavors of late harvest Riesling harmonize beautifully with the sweetness of churros, creating a decadent pairing that's perfect for dessert.
3. Pedro Ximénez Sherry: This intensely sweet and syrupy sherry boasts flavors of raisins, figs, and caramel, making it an ideal match for the caramelized exterior of churros. The complex flavors of Pedro Ximénez sherry add depth and richness to the pairing.
4. Tawny Port: With its nutty and caramelized notes, tawny port complements the cinnamon-spiced sweetness of churros. The velvety texture of the port enhances the indulgent experience of enjoying churros.
5. Brachetto d'Acqui: This sparkling red wine from Italy offers bright fruit flavors and a touch of sweetness, making it a delightful pairing with churros. Its refreshing acidity cuts through the richness of the fried dough, creating a balanced and enjoyable combination.

B. Beer and Churros: A Surprising Match

Pairing beer with churros may seem unconventional, but the right beer can complement the flavors and textures of churros beautifully. Here are some surprising beer and churros pairings to try:

1. Stout: The roasted malt flavors and creamy texture of stout beer pair well with the cinnamon sugar coating of churros. Look for a sweet stout with notes of chocolate or coffee to enhance the dessert-like qualities of churros.

2. Belgian Tripel: The fruity esters and spicy yeast character of Belgian tripel beer contrast with the sweetness of churros, creating a dynamic flavor combination. The effervescence of the tripel cleanses the palate between bites of churros, refreshing the taste buds.

3. Wheat Beer: The light and refreshing nature of wheat beer provides a pleasant contrast to the richness of churros. Look for a wheat beer with citrusy or floral notes to complement the cinnamon-spiced flavors of churros.

4. Amber Ale: The caramel and toffee flavors of amber ale complement the caramelized exterior of churros, while the moderate bitterness balances out the sweetness. The malt-forward profile of amber ale enhances the overall indulgent experience of enjoying churros.

5. Fruit Lambic: The tartness and fruitiness of fruit lambic beer add a refreshing twist to the pairing with churros. Opt for a fruit lambic with flavors that complement the dessert, such as cherry or raspberry, for a unique and enjoyable combination.

C. Tea and Churros: Complementary Flavors

Pairing tea with churros offers a delightful combination of flavors and aromas, making it a perfect match for a cozy afternoon or evening treat. Here are some complementary tea and churros pairings to savor:

1. Chai Tea: The warm spices of chai tea, such as cinnamon,

cardamom, and cloves, complement the cinnamon sugar coating of churros. The robust flavor of chai tea enhances the indulgent experience of enjoying churros, making it a perfect pairing for dessert.

2. Earl Grey Tea: The citrusy bergamot flavor of Earl Grey tea provides a refreshing contrast to the richness of churros. The floral aroma and briskness of Earl Grey tea cleanse the palate between bites of churros, allowing you to fully appreciate the flavors of both.

3. Green Tea: The grassy and vegetal notes of green tea offer a light and refreshing pairing with churros. Green tea's mild flavor profile allows the sweetness of churros to shine through, while its subtle astringency balances out the richness of the fried dough.

4. Rooibos Tea: The naturally sweet and nutty flavor of rooibos tea complements the caramelized exterior of churros. Rooibos tea's caffeine-free profile makes it a great option for enjoying with dessert any time of day.

5. Honeybush Tea: Similar to rooibos tea, honeybush tea boasts a naturally sweet and slightly floral flavor that pairs well with the sweetness of churros. Its smooth and mellow profile makes it a soothing choice for savoring alongside churros.

These tea and churros pairings offer a delightful combination of flavors and aromas, allowing you to fully enjoy the indulgent experience of savoring churros with your favorite cup of tea.

Chapter (19) Churros Candy Bar Cultural Significance

A. Churros in Literature, Art, and Film

Churros have made appearances in various forms of cultural expression, including literature, art, and film, where they often symbolize indulgence, comfort, and community. Here are some examples of how churros have been depicted in cultural works:

1. Literature: Churros have been mentioned in literature as a symbol of warmth and comfort. In some stories, characters bond over shared experiences of enjoying churros, highlighting their role in fostering connections and relationships.
2. Art: Churros have been depicted in paintings, illustrations, and other forms of visual art, often portrayed in scenes of bustling markets, lively street vendors, or cozy cafes. These artistic representations capture the vibrancy and allure of churros as a beloved culinary tradition.
3. Film: Churros have made memorable appearances in films, where they are often portrayed as a nostalgic treat or a source of joy and celebration. Whether enjoyed as a snack at a carnival, a romantic gesture between lovers, or a comforting indulgence during difficult times, churros play a significant role in cinematic storytelling.

B. Churros Traditions and Festivals Around the World

Churros hold cultural significance in many countries around the world, where they are celebrated as part of traditional festivals and culinary traditions. Here are some examples of churros traditions and festivals:

1. Spain: Churros are deeply ingrained in Spanish culture, where

they are often enjoyed as a breakfast or snack, particularly dipped in thick hot chocolate. In Spain, churros are a staple at festivals, fairs, and street markets, where they are freshly fried and served piping hot to eager revelers.

2. Mexico: Churros are a beloved dessert in Mexico, where they are commonly enjoyed with a dusting of cinnamon sugar or filled with sweet fillings like caramel or chocolate. Churros can be found at celebrations and special occasions throughout Mexico, including weddings, birthdays, and religious festivals.

3. United States: Churros have become a popular treat in the United States, where they are often sold at amusement parks, fairs, and street food vendors. In addition to traditional churros, American variations include churro ice cream sandwiches, churro bites, and churro-inspired desserts.

4. South America: Churros are enjoyed throughout South America, where they are often served with dulce de leche or fruit sauces. In countries like Argentina and Chile, churros are a common street food, enjoyed by people of all ages.

C. Churros Candy Bar as a Symbol of Unity and Celebration

The Churros Candy Bar represents more than just a delicious dessert—it embodies the spirit of unity, celebration, and cultural diversity. By combining the beloved flavors of churros with a modern twist, the Churros Candy Bar brings people together to share in the joy of indulgence and creativity.

As a symbol of unity, the Churros Candy Bar celebrates the rich tapestry of cultural influences that contribute to its creation. Whether inspired by traditional recipes from Spain, Mexico, or other parts of the world, each variation of the Churros Candy Bar reflects the unique flavors and traditions of its cultural heritage.

Furthermore, the Churros Candy Bar serves as a beacon of celebration, bringing people together to mark special occasions, share cherished memories, and create new traditions. Whether enjoyed at weddings, birthday parties, or cultural festivals, the Churros Candy Bar sparks joy and camaraderie among all who partake in its sweet delights.

In essence, the Churros Candy Bar transcends culinary boundaries to become a symbol of inclusivity, diversity, and the universal joy of indulging in a delicious treat with loved ones.

Chapter (20) Churros Candy Bar Community Engagement

A. Hosting Churros Candy Bar Fundraisers

Hosting churros candy bar fundraisers can be a fun and delicious way to raise funds for charitable causes or community organizations. Here's how you can organize a successful churros candy bar fundraiser:

1. Choose a Cause: Select a charitable cause or organization that you want to support with your fundraiser, such as a local charity, school program, or community initiative.

2. Secure a Venue: Find a suitable venue for your fundraiser, such as a school cafeteria, community center, or outdoor park. Make sure to obtain any necessary permits or permissions for hosting the event.

3. Gather Supplies: Gather all the necessary supplies for making churros candy bars, including ingredients, cooking equipment, serving utensils, and packaging materials.

4. Recruit Volunteers: Recruit volunteers to help with various tasks, such as cooking, serving, cashiering, and cleanup. Encourage community members, friends, and family to get involved and contribute their time and skills to the fundraiser.

5. Promote the Event: Use various marketing channels to promote your churros candy bar fundraiser, such as social media, flyers, posters, email newsletters, and word-of-mouth. Highlight the cause you're supporting and the delicious treats that will be available at the event.

6. Set Up the Event: Set up stations for making and serving churros candy bars, as well as a cashier station for collecting donations. Decorate the venue with festive decorations and signage to create a welcoming atmosphere.

7. Sell Churros Candy Bars: Start making and selling churros

candy bars to event attendees, offering a variety of flavors and toppings to choose from. Encourage guests to make donations in exchange for their sweet treats.

8. Engage with Attendees: Interact with event attendees, share information about the cause you're supporting, and thank them for their participation and support. Consider hosting games, raffles, or other activities to keep guests entertained and engaged throughout the event.

9. Collect Donations: Collect donations from attendees throughout the fundraiser, and provide opportunities for people to contribute additional funds beyond their churros purchases.

10. Express Gratitude: After the fundraiser, express gratitude to everyone who participated, volunteered, or made donations. Share updates on the amount raised and how it will be used to support the chosen cause or organization.

B. Collaborating with Local Businesses for Churros Events

Collaborating with local businesses for churros events can help create exciting opportunities for community engagement and support. Here's how you can collaborate with local businesses for churros events:

1. Identify Potential Partners: Reach out to local bakeries, cafes, restaurants, food trucks, or grocery stores that specialize in churros or similar desserts. Look for businesses that share your commitment to supporting the community and charitable causes.

2. Propose Collaboration: Present your idea for a churros event collaboration to potential partners, highlighting the mutual benefits of working together. Emphasize how the event can help promote their business, attract new customers, and contribute to a worthy cause.

3. Discuss Details: Collaborate with the chosen business to plan

the details of the churros event, such as the date, location, menu offerings, pricing, and promotion strategy. Determine how proceeds from the event will be shared or donated to the chosen cause or organization.

4. Promote the Event: Use both partners' marketing channels to promote the churros event to the local community. Leverage social media, email newsletters, website announcements, and in-store signage to generate excitement and encourage attendance.

5. Coordinate Logistics: Coordinate logistics for the churros event, including setting up the venue, preparing the churros, managing sales and payments, and ensuring a smooth flow of customers. Work together with the partner business to provide a seamless and enjoyable experience for attendees.

6. Engage with Attendees: Engage with event attendees, share information about the cause or organization being supported, and encourage them to participate in the event. Offer samples, promotions, or special deals to attract more customers and increase sales.

7. Evaluate Success: After the event, evaluate its success based on factors such as attendance, sales, customer feedback, and funds raised for the chosen cause or organization. Take note of lessons learned and areas for improvement for future collaborations.

C. Sharing Churros Candy Bar Recipes with Food Banks and Shelters

Sharing churros candy bar recipes with food banks and shelters can provide individuals and families in need with access to delicious and comforting treats. Here's how you can share churros candy bar recipes with food banks and shelters:

1. Contact Local Organizations: Reach out to local food banks, homeless shelters, soup kitchens, or community centers to

inquire about their interest in receiving recipe donations. Explain how the recipes can help enhance their meal offerings and provide enjoyment to those they serve.

2. Provide Recipe Resources: Offer to provide printed copies of churros candy bar recipes, along with any necessary cooking instructions or tips for preparing the treats. Consider creating recipe cards or pamphlets that can be easily distributed and shared with clients or volunteers.

3. Offer Cooking Workshops or Demos: Offer to conduct cooking workshops or demonstrations at food banks or shelters to teach staff, volunteers, or clients how to make churros candy bars from scratch. Provide hands-on guidance and support to ensure successful preparation and execution of the recipes.

4. Donate Ingredients or Supplies: Consider donating ingredients or cooking supplies needed to make churros candy bars, such as flour, sugar, cinnamon, cooking oil, or piping bags. Your contributions can help alleviate the financial burden on food banks and shelters and make it easier for them to prepare the recipes.

5. Encourage Creativity: Encourage food bank staff, volunteers, or clients to get creative with the churros candy bar recipes by experimenting with different flavors, fillings, or toppings. Provide suggestions for variations and adaptations that can cater to diverse tastes and dietary preferences.

6. Collect Feedback: Collect feedback from food bank clients, shelter residents, or staff members about their experience making and enjoying the churros candy bar recipes. Use their input to refine and improve the recipes and tailor them to better meet the needs and preferences of the community.

7. Share Success Stories: Share success stories and testimonials from food bank clients, shelter residents, or volunteers who have enjoyed making and eating churros candy bars. Highlight

the positive impact of the recipes in bringing joy, comfort, and a sense of community to those in need.

Sweet Endings

A. Churros Candy Bar Trivia and Fun Facts

- Churros are believed to have originated in Spain, where shepherds would fry dough to cook easily while tending their sheep.
- The name "churro" is thought to have derived from the Spanish word "churra," referring to the type of sheep commonly found in Spain.
- Churros are popular in many countries around the world, including Spain, Mexico, the Philippines, and the United States, each with its own unique variations and serving styles.
- In Mexico, churros are often served with a dipping sauce called cajeta, made from caramelized goat's milk.
- In Spain, churros are traditionally enjoyed for breakfast or as a snack, often dipped in thick, rich hot chocolate.
- Churros gained popularity in the United States during the 19th and 20th centuries, especially in areas with large Hispanic populations such as California and Texas.
- Churros have become a popular dessert at theme parks, carnivals, and fairs, where they are often served freshly fried and coated in cinnamon sugar.
- Churros are versatile and can be served in various forms, including traditional sticks, loops, spirals, and filled with various sweet or savory fillings.
- Churros are often associated with celebrations and festivals, such as Cinco de Mayo in Mexico and Las Fallas in Spain, where they are enjoyed as a festive treat.

B. Final Thoughts and Farewell

As we conclude this journey through the delectable world of churros candy bars, I hope you've been inspired to explore the endless possibilities of these delightful treats. Whether you're indulging in classic churros with chocolate drizzle or getting creative with unique variations and mashups, churros are sure to bring joy to any occasion.

From traditional recipes to vegan and gluten-free options, churros offer something for everyone to enjoy. So gather your friends and family, set up a churros candy bar station, and let your imagination run wild as you create sweet memories together.

Thank you for joining me on this culinary adventure. May your churros be crispy, your fillings be flavorful, and your dipping sauces be decadent. Until we meet again, farewell and happy churro-making!